Other giftbooks by Helen Exley:
To a very special Grandmother   To a very special Granddaughter
To a very special Grandson   An Illustrated Grandmother's Notebook

Published simultaneously in 1997 by Exley Giftbooks in the USA and Exley Publications
Ltd in Great Britain.

12 11 10 9 8 7

ISBN 1-85015-852-5

A copy of the CIP data is available from the British Library on request. All rights
reserved. No part of this publication may be reproduced or transmitted in any form or by
any means, electronic or mechanical, including photocopy, recording or any information
storage and retrieval system without permission in writing from the publisher.

Edited and pictures selected by Helen Exley.
Pictures researched by Image Select International.
Typeset by Delta, Watford.
Printed and bound in China.

Exley Publications Ltd, 16 Chalk Hill, Watford, Herts WD1 4BN, UK.
Exley Publications LLC, 232 Madison Avenue, Suite 1409, NY 10016, USA.

Acknowledgements: The publishers are grateful for permission to reproduce copyright material.
Whilst every effort has been made to trace copyright holders, the publishers would be pleased to
hear from any not here acknowledged. NELL DUNN: Extracts from *Grandmothers Talking to Nell
Dunn*, © 1991 Nell Dunn. Reprinted by permission of Curtis Brown Group Ltd, London. RUTH
GOODE: Extracts from *A Book For Grandmothers*, © Ruth Goode 1977. Reprinted by permission of
Curtis Brown Ltd. LILY MUNRO: Extract from a private letter paying tribute to her grandson.
GRACE NICHOLS: "Granny Granny Please Comb My Hair" in *Families*, © Grace Nichols 1988.
Reprinted by permission of MacDonald Publishers. BARTY PHILLIPS: Extract from *Your New
Grandchild* by Barty Phillips. Reprinted by permission of Piatkus Books. FRIEDA McREYNOLDS:
Extract from "A Grateful Granddaughter" in *Grandmothers Are Like Snowflakes... No Two Are Alike*
ed. Janet Lanese. Reprinted by permission of Bantam Doubleday Dell Publishing, Inc. DORCAS
MOYER: Extract from "My Grandmother Is..." in *Grandmothers Are Like Snowflakes... No Two Are
Alike* ed. Janet Lanese. Permission as above. KATE RUSHIN: Extract from "Family Tree" in *Double
Stitch* ed. Patricia Bell-Scott et al., 1991. LOIS WYSE: Extract from "Inheritance" in *Grandmothers
Are Special People*. Reprinted by permission of Antioch Publishing Co.

Picture credits: Exley Publications is very grateful to the following individuals and organizations
for permission to reproduce their pictures: Alinari (ALI), Archiv Fur Kunst (AKG), Art Resource
(AR), Artworks (AW), The Bridgeman Art Library (BAL), Bulloz (BU), Chris Beetles Gallery
(CBG), Christie's Images (CI), Edimedia (EDM), Fine Art Photographic Library (FAP), Scala (SCA),
Sotheby's Transparency Library (STL), Statens Konstmuseer (SKM), The Image Bank (TIB): Cover:
© 1999 Sir William Rothenstein, *Spring – The Morning Room*, BAL; title-page: George Bernard
O'Neill, *Family Treasures*, STL; page 7: © 1997 Eugenio Zampighi, *Her First Lesson*, City Museum
and Art Gallery, Stoke-on-Trent/BAL; page 8: U. Boccioni, *The Sister on the Balcony*, ALI; pages
10/11: Camille Corot, *The Road*, AR; page 13: © 1997 Karl Moll, *At Breakfast*, AKG; page 15: George
Smith, *Here's Granny*, FAP; page 17: Robert Gantt Steele, *Grandmother and Granddaughters Baking*,
TIB; page 19 © 1997 Sir John Lavery, *A Young Woman Pushing a Baby in a Pram*, CI; page 21: © 1997
Carlo Magno, *Parang Kahapon Lamang*, Philippine collection; page 22: © 1997 Peter Fiore, AW; page
24: Michele Gordigiani, *Portrait of Gabriella*, SCA; page 26: Alessandro Sani, *Her Favorite Tune*, FAP;
page 29: © 1997 Eduardo G. Perrnoud Jr, *Market Square*, Philippine collection; page 30: © 1997
Gladys Rockmore Davis, *The Hair Ribbon*, Private Collection/BAL; page 32: Anders Zorn, *Stickande
kulla*, SKM; page 35: Laura W. Waring, *Jessie R. Fauset*, National Museum of American Art; page
37: Leghe Suthers, *Dame Trimmer*, Whitford & Hughes, London/BAL; page 38: CBG; page 41: ©
1997 Childe Hassam, *A Rainy Day in Boston*, BAL; page 43: Thomas Waterman Wood, *Sunday
Morning*, National Museum of American Art; page 45: Harriet Backer, *By Lamplight*, Ramus
Mayers Samlinger, Bergen/BAL; page 46: Carl Larsson, *Mor och barn*, SKM; page 48: © 1997
Wassili Dmitrijewitsch Polenow, *Grandmother's Garden*, AKG; page 51: © 1997 Archipov Abraham
Epimowitch, *Countrywoman in a green apron*, SCA; page 52: Umberto Boccioni, *Woman Reading*,
Museo d'Arte Moderna, Venice/BAL; page 54: William Henry Midwood, *Cottage Interior*, Roy
Miles Gallery/BAL; page 57: Pissarro, BU; page 58: © 1997 Jose Blanco, *Golden Harvest*, Philippine
collection; page 60: © 1997 Frederico D. Estrada, *Light in the Dark*, Philippine collection.

THE LOVE BETWEEN

Grandmothers and Grandchildren

EDITED BY

HELEN EXLEY

NEW YORK • WATFORD, UK

MY GRANDDAUGHTER IS...

... a bell of laughter shattering
the morning sun
... a crystal gift of tears for me
to wipe away
... a present joy that now is more
than I can ever say
... a promise of a future when
my days are done.

DORCAS MOYER

"... her [grandchildren] couldn't
defeat her. Or disappoint her. Or
prove anything – anything good
or bad – about her. And I saw
her free of ambition, free of the
need to control, free of anxiety.
Free, as she liked to put it
– to enjoy."

JUDITH VIORST, b.1931

"Grandmother-grandchild relationships are simple. Grandmas are short on criticism and long on love."

GRANDMA JAN

"Grandmas are the sort of people that are absolutely full up when there is one cream cake left on the plate."

BEVERLEY ANN THOULD,
AGE 12

"We should all have one person who knows how to bless us despite the evidence, Grandmother was that person to me...."

PHYLLIS THEROUX

"The kind sweet souls who love, cherish, inspire and protect their grandchildren are not guardian angels; they are grandmothers."

BETTYE "MI MI" FLYNN

"Grandparents somehow sprinkle a sense of stardust over grandchildren."

ALEX HALEY

*"I like my grandma because she likes me from
her heart."*

CHISA KIKUMORI, AGE 8

*"I'm a flower, Poa, a flower opening and reaching
for the sun. You are the sun, Grandma, you are the sun
in my life."*

KITTY TSUI, FROM "POA POA IS LIVING BREATHING LIGHT"

"No one... who has not known that inestimable privilege can possibly realize what good fortune it is to grow up in a home where there are grandparents."

SUZANNE LAFOLLETTE

"... everyone needs to have access both to grandparents and grandchildren in order to be a full human being."

MARGARET MEAD
(1901-1978),
FROM "BLACKBERRY WINTER"

FROM A GRATEFUL GRANDDAUGHTER

For as long as I can remember you
were always there
To teach me how to love others,
and how to love myself...
And to look for the good in everyone.
You were always there to listen,
to hold my hand, and to hug me.
Your joy for life and nurturing care
Have been a major influence
in my life.

Thank you for being my grandmother.

FRIEDA McREYNOLDS

"The only ones who don't notice when your hair starts graying, your face is sagging, and your waistline is disappearing are your grandchildren and the family dog."

GRANDMA JAN,
FROM "GRANDMOTHERS ARE LIKE SNOWFLAKES... "

"Grandmother and grandchild discussing a common interest are exactly the same age."

DUANE BIRCH

"I don't go along with all this talk of a generation gap. We're all contemporaries. There is only a difference in memories, that's all."

W.H. AUDEN (1907-1973)

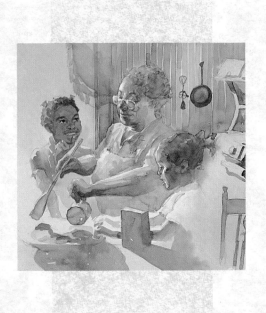

"I sing to him, Nell, and I love him.
I've never loved anyone so much.
The baby's my life now. He's my new life.
I've never loved like this."

JOY, FROM "GRANDMOTHERS TALKING TO NELL DUNN"

"She has the biggest blue eyes I have ever seen and a determined personality. That is to say, she knows what she likes and in her quiet way will get it. She likes pretty things and peaceful things. She likes to think about what she wants to say before she says it. She likes things to be neat and tidy and she likes pretty clothes – she won't wear tracksuits or jeans and her shoes must be shiny.... My granddaughter makes me proud to be a grandmother. She has removed from me the fear of growing old. She is my companion and my friend. I hope she knows this. I think she is sure to."

FROM "YOUR NEW GRANDCHILD",
BY BARTY PHILLIPS

"The nice thing about her, is that she says that I've got two homes, my home and their home."

JULIA GAMBOLD, AGE 9,
FROM "GRANDMAS AND GRANDPAS"

"Grandma's home is her grandchildren's second home, a sort of security blanket they can escape to when the world is unfriendly."

GRANDMA JAN,
FROM "GRANDMOTHERS ARE LIKE SNOWFLAKES... NO TWO ARE ALIKE"

"Of all my childhood memories, days spent in my grandparents' house are the happiest. I know now that they were poor, but to us they were rich – love, laughter, bedtime stories, cuddles by the fire, songs round the piano, hunks of bread and dripping on a cold morning – wealth indeed."

ROSEMARY WELLS,
FROM "YOUR GRANDCHILD AND YOU"

"I loved their home. Everything smelled older, worn but safe; the food aroma had baked itself into the furniture."

SUSAN STRASBERG, FROM "BITTERSWEET"

"Most grandmas
have a touch of the scallywag."

HELEN THOMSON, b.1943

"It's very hard on you, when you are struggling
to learn the rules – even of rebellion –
to be saddled with a grandma
who has outlived those rules.
And sits on a wall when her feet ache.
And laughs too loudly in the cinema.
And talks to strangers at bus shelters.
And to waiters."

PAM BROWN, b.1928

"I cultivate
Being Uppity
It's Something
My Gramom taught me."

KATE RUSHIN, FROM "FAMILY TREE"

"Each one of our grandchildren is a fresh, unique experience, a new personality, a small but definite individual with whom we can forge a bond. If we are shy with babies, soon enough we find them toddlers, conversationalists on the telephone, crayon artists sending us pictures, school children writing us awkwardly formed words in block letters and original spellings, teenagers confiding to us their adolescent joys and griefs. We can enter their lives at any stage with which we feel comfortable. And we enter with an ideal introduction, a passport second only to that of their parents. We are their grandparents."

RUTH GOODE, b.1905,
FROM "A BOOK FOR GRANDMOTHERS"

"Parents give grandmas solemn lectures before they take you out. Some of it gets through – but not much. They are too busy planning mischief."

JENNY DE VRIES

"Grandmas mustn't take sides – but there's nothing to stop them winking."

CLARA ORTEGA, b.1955

"When grandparents enter the door, discipline flies out the window."

OGDEN NASH (1902-1971)

"My grandma doesn't make me eat my vegetables and when my parents have gone out of the room she eats my cabbage for me."

GEMMA BEEVERS, AGE 9,
FROM "TO THE WORLD'S BEST GRANDMA"

"To show a child what has once delighted you, to find the child's delight added to your own, so that there is now a double delight seen in the glow of trust and affection, this is happiness."

J.B. PRIESTLEY

"... nothing can ever take the place of a child running in and out of your home – or of a granny's lap to snuggle into."

ROSEMARY WELLS,
FROM "YOUR GRANDCHILD AND YOU"

"Grandmothers and grandchildren have a lot in common.
They are inclined to straggle behind on walks. They doze off at unexpected moments. They like fancy cakes. They are very fond of cats and know how to talk to them. They are given to falling over.
They get the giggles."

PAM BROWN, b.1928

Granny Granny
please comb my hair
you always take your time
you always take such care

You put me to sit on a cushion
between your knees
you rub a little coconut oil
parting gentle as a breeze

... Granny
you have all the time in the world
and when you're finished
you always turn my head and say
"Now who's a nice girl."

GRACE NICHOLS

"A grandmother is a luxury most of us can afford when we are very young. They say that they are our mother's or father's mother — but we only half believe them — for they belong to us. Their whole existence is dictated by our own.

They do have houses and cups and saucers and fruit cake and gardens and cats. But it is as if all they possess is on stand-by, waiting for us to visit.

They are there to tell us stories, sing us songs, talk about The Long Ago, give us Surprizzles, keep our secrets, show us how to do things, tie up shoelaces — with a bit of pulling. And trail behind with us when our parents are shopping.

They are there to be hugged and snuggled, made cups of invisible tea, sung to and wrapped up in blankets.

They are there to love us.

And to be loved back."

PAM BROWN, b.1928

"I remember very clearly, it was when she was six weeks old, I suddenly thought, 'I've fallen in love!' I hadn't felt it before then, but you know when you fall in love that awful lurching feeling, that stomach-turning-over feeling, I suddenly had it with Katie."

DIANA, FROM "GRANDMOTHERS TALKING TO NELL DUNN"

"The clock ticks. The fire splutters. The cat sings.
There's a knock. Open the door – and there is a smile and outstretched arms and a splodgy kiss and a rush of feet. And a day transformed."

PAM BROWN, b.1928

"It doesn't take long to learn that it is the simple things children love best; and their joy brings these experiences into the importance they truly deserve. Sharing laughter and wonder and fun with children, seeing the world through their eyes, helps me to understand what is really important in life and what is not."

J.L. NIXON,
FROM "THE GRANDMOTHER'S BOOK"

"What Cato gives me is the sheer pleasure of living. He reminds me that there isn't so much to it all, that actually a good breakfast, a nice walk, a new word, good weather, a new hat – everything – is just outrageously delightful, and that it's as simple as that, and all those things that take enormous effort are not necessarily where our satisfaction comes from. The greatest surprise for me is that after seeking satisfaction in so many places it can be so easy, so before my nose, and over such simple matters. It is valuing things as they are."

NINA, FROM "GRANDMOTHERS TALKING
TO NELL DUNN"

"Every Saturday I visit my granny and we discuss what we did during the week. I talk to her about everything, she understands me. When I am sad she cheers me up, and we have a laugh together. She looked after me since I was a baby. She is my best friend."

MAIRE FEENEY, AGE 9,
FROM "TO THE WORLD'S BEST GRANDMA"

"I watch through the window. Grandma and grandchild in the vegetable garden, working their way down the rows. Heads bent together, small face peering, old hand pointing. They straighten, nod their heads. What are they discussing? The ravages of cabbage whites? The need to net the fruit? The sturdiest way to fix the bean poles? On they go. Sixty years between them. Gardeners both."

PAM BROWN, b.1928

"An old woman with the soul of a young girl who opened her heart to me, because she felt we were kindred spirits.
She recreated the world, making it a wonderful place in which everything might happen. In which a tree or a stone was so much more than what we could see with our eyes. She showed me how the veins in leaves were alive and pulsating. And she was the first to tell me that plants cried out when you hurt them."

LIV ULLMANN,
ABOUT HER GRANDMOTHER, FROM
"CHANGING"

"If a child is to keep alive his inborn sense of wonder without any such gift from the fairies, he needs the companionship of at least one adult who can share it, rediscovering with him the joy, excitement, and mystery of the world we live in."

RACHEL CARSON (1907-1964)

"I was her little shadow, and that was just the way I wanted it. Goggy was two hundred years old and would let me chase her all around the big old house and tickle her. When I caught her, I didn't tickle her too hard because she could've broken."

CAROL BURNETT

"You can get a lot more mileage out of a grandma if you tell her there's a cup of tea ahead."

PAM BROWN, b.1928

"Never lift your grandma's eyelids to see if she's awake."

MARION C. GARRETTY, b.1917

"Grannies' hearts are willing, but their feet give out."

ROSANNE AMBROSE BROWN

"I would like to pay tribute to a most thoughtful loving grandson. I am retired. I lost my husband nearly three years ago. My grandson was seven years old when my husband died. He has not missed one day coming to see me. I thrill when he says, 'Nan are you all right, anything you want?' I have not been very well this winter, so John has been staying at weekends. He puts the bottle in bed for me and, before he goes to sleep, he says, 'Wake me Nana if you want anything.' He has given me so much love my husband used to say we were like two peas in a pod. I think he is wonderful. He has made me so happy I have no need to feel so lonely, and when he says, 'I will put a record on' we dance. I get a lovely feeling he makes me want to hug him, and I do. The street where I live all the people are like myself all retired, and he always asks if there is any shopping to do and if he sees them carrying their shopping bags he takes them off them. When we have snow he clears it off for everybody, and they think a lot of John. I think I am the most luckiest nan in the world."

LILY MUNRO

"A grandma is the person you go to when no one else will listen."

MAYA V. PATEL

"When I fall and cut my knee she takes me in and laughs. I love her gentle loving touch, it makes me feel so safe."

KAREN WILSON, AGE 10

"She's the perfect woman for advice. When I'm sad she'll always be sitting in her comfy chair."

SARAH BREARLEY, AGE 11,
FROM "TO THE WORLD'S BEST GRANDMA"

"When we run out of ideas, when we run out of steam, when we run out of hope – who has ideas and steam and hope to spare? Grandma!"

PAM BROWN, b.1928

"Grandma has got a bad leg, so she can't walk around without her cane. I can sit on her lap, though, and she tells me stories about when she was young and I can cuddle up with her. It sounds weird, but I like to snuggle into her and smell her and rub her arm in my face. She is so cosy. She can't walk too well, but she can talk. And she is the best back-rubber in the world."

PATTY, AGE 7

"I grasped her hand like a common consoling friend and felt, immediately, the grim forbidding strength of her, undiminished all these years."

LOUISE ERDRICH, b.1954

"[My grandmother] was the one member of my immediate family who most understood me, or so I thought at the time. Looking back, I think it was not so much her understanding as it was the sheer force of her encouragement that helped me through those years...."

**LINDA SUNSHINE,
FROM "TO GRANDMOTHER WITH LOVE"**

"Her manner of storytelling evoked tenderness and mystery as she put her face close to mine and fixed me with her big, believing eyes. Thus was the strength that was developing in me directly infused from her."

MAXIM GORKY

"*Grandchildren are the best excuse I know to do all the undignified things that are so much fun.*"

MARION C. GARRETTY, b.1917

"*We danced on and on, unequal partners who in those moments absolutely loved all the inequalities about us, the jokiness, the seriousness. My grandmother was singing: her voice was loud and clear. She spun me for a long time. Our heads thrown back, legs stepping, arms pumping, our fingers intertwined.*"

MARCIE HERSHMAN

"*A car draws up. Doors bang. Shrill voices. Scampering feet. A thunderous knocking. 'Happy birthday Granny!' Now it's begun.*"

PAM BROWN, b.1928

To forget one's ancestors is to be a brook without a source, a tree without a root.

CHINESE PROVERB

"Young people need something stable to hang on to – a culture connection, a sense of their own past, a hope for their own future. Most of all, they need what grandparents can give them...."

JAY KESLER,
FROM "GRANDPARENTING: THE AGONY AND THE ECSTASY"

"The history of our grandparents is remembered not with rose petals but in the laughter and tears of their children and their children's children. It is into us that the lives of grandparents have gone. It is in us that their history becomes a future."

CHARLES & ANN MORSE,
FROM "LET THIS BE A DAY FOR GRANDPARENTS"

*"Grandmas are always slow
but they do not mind for
they have all the time in
the world."*

MALCOLM ANDREW, AGE 10

*"Grandma always made you
feel she had been waiting to
see just you all day and now
the day was complete."*

MARCY DEMAREE

*"Grandmas and grandpas
have nothing to do but
talk to you."*

CATHERINE MELLORS,
FROM
"GRANDMAS AND GRANDPAS"

"They link us to our own motherhood and childhood years, to our parents and grandparents and the stories we remember of times even earlier than those. And they link us to the future as well. They give us a vested interest in the world in which they will live. They make us aware of the world in which we are living today and helping to create for tomorrow."

RUTH GOODE, b.1905,
FROM "A BOOK FOR GRANDMOTHERS"

"I love to hold your hands, Grandma. They lead me back to the time before I began. They keep me safe against the world outside."

PAMELA DUGDALE

"I was an angel in her eyes, no matter what the facts were, no matter what anyone else happened to think."

JUDY LANGFORD CARTER

"My nanny is like a treasure to me and I keep her safe in a special place in my heart. Nanny has me under a type of spell to keep me good, it cannot be broken."

VICTORIA GRAHAM, AGE 8,
FROM "TO THE WORLD'S BEST GRANDMA"

"Many times in the warmth of our hogan, Grandmother spoke of her days as a young girl, emphasizing the need for me to listen carefully so that I could learn from her experiences as well as understand her reasons for the harsh treatment she gave me while learning the ways of The People. She made the best of life without complaint. She was taught to do that; it was the way of her people."

RAY BALDWIN LOUIS

"A child needs a grandparent, anybody's grandparent, to grow a little more securely into an unfamiliar world."

CHARLES & ANN MORSE,
FROM "LET THIS BE A DAY FOR GRANDPARENTS"

"If the very old will remember, the very young will listen."

CHIEF DAN GEORGE